Lost Lear

Dan Colley

methuen | drama

LONDON · NEW YORK · OXFORD · NEW DELHI · SYDNEY

METHUEN DRAMA

Bloomsbury Publishing Plc, 50 Bedford Square, London, WC1B 3DP, UK
Bloomsbury Publishing Inc, 1359 Broadway, New York, NY 10018, USA
Bloomsbury Publishing Ireland, 29 Earlsfort Terrace, Dublin 2,
D02 AY28, Ireland

BLOOMSBURY, METHUEN DRAMA and the Methuen
Drama logo are trademarks of Bloomsbury Publishing Plc.

First published in Great Britain 2025

Cover design: Jade Barnett

Photography by Patricio Cassinoni

Illustration by Sarah Maloney

A catalogue record for this book is available from the British Library.

Library of Congress Control Number: 2025941906

ISBN: PB: 978-1-3505-9636-8
ePDF: 978-1-3505-9637-5
eBook: 978-1-3505-9638-2

Series: Modern Plays

Typeset by Mark Heslington Ltd, Scarborough, North Yorkshire
Printed and bound in Great Britain

For product safety related questions contact
productsafety@bloomsbury.com.

To find out more about our authors and books visit
www.bloomsbury.com and sign up for our newsletters.

Lost Lear was a co-production of Riverbank Arts Centre and Mermaid Arts Centre. In 2022 it previewed at Riverbank Arts Centre, premiered at the Dublin Theatre Festival and transferred to the Mermaid Arts Centre. A 2023 revival toured to Riverbank Arts Centre, Newbridge; The Everyman, Cork; Westival, Westport; The Town Hall Theatre, Galway; Project Arts Centre, Dublin; The Hawkswell, Sligo; The Ramor, Cavan; Mermaid Arts Centre, Bray; Draíocht, Blanchardstown; The Civic Theatre, Tallaght. A 2024 revival toured to Aotearoa New Zealand Festival of the Arts, Wellington. A 2025 revival toured to the John and Joan Mullen Center for the Arts, Philadelphia (presented by the Center for Irish Studies, Villanova); and the Traverse Theatre, Edinburgh.

Lost Lear was created in the context of Dan Colley's residency at Riverbank Arts Centre, funded by the Arts Council | An Chomhairle Ealaíon and Kildare Arts Services. Development was supported by Fishamble: The New Play Company's New Play Clinic.

Directed & Conceived by	Dan Colley
Text by	Dan Colley, William Shakespeare & The Cast
Music by	Daniel McAuley
Set Design	Andrew Clancy
Lighting Design	Suzie Cummins
Costume Design	Cherie White
Sound Design	Kevin Gleeson
Video Design	Ross Ryder
Dramaturg	Gavin Kostick
Assistant Director	Joy Nesbitt
Producer	Matthew Smyth

Original Cast
Venetia Bowe, Peter Daly, Manus Halligan

Original Ensemble
Clodagh O'Farrell, Em Ormonde

Presentation at the Traverse Theatre, Edinburgh Fringe 2025

Cast

Liam	Manus Halligan
Conor	Peter Daly / Gus McDonagh
Joy	Venetia Bowe
Ensemble	Clodagh O'Farrell & Em Ormonde

Stage Manager	Iain Synott
Chief AV	Laura Rainsford
Production Manager	Eoin Kilkenny
Graphic Design	Sarah Moloney
Lead image	Patricio Cassinoni
Production Photography	Ste Murray
Public Relations	Ruth Marsh
Producers	Matthew Smyth & Ois O'Donoghue

Lost Lear is co-produced by Riverbank Arts Centre and Mermaid Arts Centre. It was funded by the Arts Council | An Chomhairle Ealaíon and supported by Fishamble: The New Play Company's New Play Clinic.

Touring supported by Culture Ireland.

Alzheimer Scotland Helpline

Volunteers on the Helpline can provide information right away if you have any questions or concerns, as well as send out free information to carers, family members or people with dementia.

Freephone: 0808 808 3000 or email *helpline@alzscot.org*

Author's Note by Dan Colley

For a time, my grandmother lived in a care home for people with dementia. In that home there was a row of fake shop fronts designed to make a section of corridor look like an Irish streetscape from the early 20th century. It was intended to comfort the residents with, what the designers imagined, was a familiar environment from their childhoods.

I learned about features of other care homes with a similar aim; a train carriage with screens for windows that displayed footage of passing landscape; a prop phone with the recorded voice of a loved one that could be conversed with again and again; a care home designed like an indoor village, with avenues of clapboard houses, a town square and lighting that mimicked the change from day to night – reminiscent of a film set or immersive theatre.

In Oliver James' book *Contented Dementia*, I learned about a practice that goes a step further. He describes Penny Garner's SPECAL method, which asks carers to identify a happy, fulfilling memory from the person's pre-dementia past, and actively work to keep them living in that memory.

Garner would say that from the point of view of a person with dementia, it's not the memory loss that's confusing, it's all the people talking nonsense that couldn't possibly be true.

From the family carers I spoke to, it seems most people lie. It's a fact of caring for someone who, at times, has a completely different understanding of the world to you. Not all carers go as far as to identify and maintain a bespoke immersive fiction, but most carers allow falsehoods to become true.

I spoke to people with dementia. Many wanted to impress upon me that dementia is not the end of you. It's a new phase. It's a more complicated life than you might have had before but it can be a good life. It's a question of how to manage it – how to maintain your relationships, your health, your dignity.

And there are as many ways to do that as there are people with dementia. No one has a perfect answer.

To my eye, that replica of a streetscape in the corridor of a care home was utterly unconvincing. I wondered what it told me about my grandmother's perception of the world that someone thought this vista would comfort her. It was a momentary insight into how someone else saw the world. It was eerily unfamiliar to me and I wondered; how do any of us live together?

Note on the Text

This text is a record of our production which was created through a devising process. In order to represent Joy's experience of the world, and the ruptures to it, we made choices about the production design and the age of the cast members. Some of these choices are referred to in the stage directions. Future productions may find other ways to achieve the same intention.

The 'box of envelopes' analogy for consciousness as an emergent property of matter was first articulated in 'I Am a Strange Loop' by Douglas Hofstadter.

Acknowledgements

Thank you to the artists who contributed to the piece over the years, including Fionnuala Gygax, Breffni Holohan, Genevieve Hulme-Beaman, Matthew Malone, Janet Moran, Gina Moxley, Clodagh O'Farrell, Rebecca O'Mara, Em Ormonde, Joy Nesbitt, Louise Stephenson and Ragnheiður Skúladóttir.

Thank you to the people who shared their experience of dementia in workshops and conversations. Members of the Irish Dementia Working Group and Dementia Carers Campaign Network; Denise Monahan, Máire-Anne Doyle, Paddy Crosbie, Susan Crampton and Richard Dolan. Judy Williams and Clodagh Whelan of the Alzheimer Society of Ireland. Christine Doey of the Contented Dementia Trust. Dr Mary Cosgrave, Dr Regina McQuillan, Dr Cathriona Russell, Dr Carol Rogan and Dr Linda Hogan.

Friends and confidants Gerry Stembridge, Sarah Byrne, Fionnuala Dillon and Carys D. Coburn. Kate Ferris and the Abbey Theatre's 'Engine Room'. Our colleagues Caroline Williams, Julie Kelleher, Willie White and Ciarán Walsh. The team from the original production, including Evie McGuinness, Sarah Purcell, Sara Gannon and Adrian Moylan.

Lost Lear

For Mary Colley

Characters

Liam
Conor
Joy
Crew/Carers

Prologue

Downstage of a curtain. **Liam** *(age mid-30s) tells the story to* **Conor** *(age mid-50s).*

Liam Ok well eh . . . there was this king . . . and he'd had a long reign. Lots of achievement and that. He was brilliant, I guess. Anyway, one day he woke up and said to himself eh . . . 'to hell with all this, I've done enough' and he made a decision.

So he threw a big dinner party and invited all the important people. Your dukes, your lords, your knights. And his daughters were there. He's got three daughters; there's Goneril, she's the eldest so she's sort of *(makes a face)*, Regan, who is, you know, the middle child type so she's kind of *(makes a face)*, and Cordelia. Cordelia is the youngest. And his favourite.

So anyway, at the end of dinner, once they've finished their apple tart and jelly or what have you, he said 'I've made a decision'.

He says he's made a decision that he's going to retire. He says, 'You are each going to have a piece of my kingdom and you . . . ' Sorry. He's saying this to his daughters now. He says he's going to retire 'and you can look after me, and my one hundred best knights, until I die'. 'Right,' he says, 'tell me how much you love me.' 'Bring me the map,' he says 'and I'll slice it up based on how I feel about your answers. Tell me how much you love me.'

So eh . . . the first one, Goneril, stands up and she's like . . . 'Blahblahblah I love you' eh and then Regan gets up and she's like 'I actually love you a little bit more than what she said.' And Lear is like 'Okookokok. Land for you. Land for you. Done.' And then Cordelia stands up and she says 'Nothing.' And the King's like 'Eh nothing?' And she says 'Nothing.' And then Lear's like 'Well nothing will come of nothing, speak again!' And she still says 'Nothing'.

So then he kicks off. He tells Cordelia she's disinherited. That she was his favourite and how his heart is broken now. He flies off the handle. He says right, Goneril, you and Regan can have the land she was going to get and now me and my friends will stay with you.

So the King anyway. He forgets about Cordelia and he and his one hundred knights and . . . oh yeah and his best friend the Fool . . . they go and stay in Goneril's house. And they are . . . they're a rambunctious lot. They are kicking back, drinking loads, smoking in doors, putting their feet up on the coffee tables, they . . . they're having a great time!

And Goneril puts up with this . . . she does. For a bit. But then eventually she's like 'I'll have no more of this, Dad. You're wearing me out.' And he's like 'Fine! I have another daughter' but then Regan says 'Yeah what Goneril said' and he's like 'but we had a deal. You can't go back on that now. That's madness!'

So then he tells them all where to go. He grabs his Fool, and he says 'come on, we're going to live out in the wild. Right? Never mind that pair, they're just . . . awful people.' So the King and the Fool they run out and they're out in this . . . massive storm. Right there's a big storm and he's shouting. And he's so angry, and eh . . . oh and the Fool, the Fool comes up him and he's like 'C'mere, would you not come into this cave here for a bit' and he's like 'No way! This storm is the only thing that makes sense!' And then . . . and then . . . he's out there and the wind is blowing and the rain is slapping him, and his beard's all wet and there's trees being uprooted . . . it's like a category five storm. And then . . . eh . . . erm . . . (*has to think now*) Oh yeah then he sees Cordelia . . . or no . . . he starts thinking about her . . . and then . . . then Cordelia just shows up. And she listens to him while he apologi . . . sorry no he doesn't apologise . . . Lear just says 'forgive me' and Cordelia says she does. And they make up. And that's Lear. (*Pause.*) You'll pick it up.

Curtain pulls back.

Act I

Retirement Party

A palace banquet hall and a rehearsal room. Preparation. Ritual. Crew. **Joy** *(age mid-30s). Costume. Makeup check.* **Conor** *is awkward in the background.*

Liam (*to* **Conor**, *low*)
It's just through here. So this is the rehearsal room. There's our star over there. So, as I said, don't ask direct questions, don't contradict, just listen, react. Best to speak when spoken to . . . ok?
(*To others.*) Laura, how we getting on there? Act one, scene one, you have it.
How are we getting on Clodagh, good to go? Costumes costumes. All good, Em?

(*To* **Joy**.) Ok Joy, shall we take a look at this?

Joy *sits on the chair centre stage. Crew crowns her.*

Joy
I've made a decision.
I've made a decision.
I've made a decision
We shall express our darker purpose.
Give me the map there. Know that we have divided
In three our kingdom: and 'tis our fast intent
To shake all cares and business from our age;
Conferring them on younger strengths, while we
Unburthen'd crawl toward death.
Tell me, my daughters, Help me make my decision. Which of you shall we say doth love us most?

Goneril – our first born – speak first!

Liam
Oh eh – (*reading*)
Sir, I love you more than words can wield the matter;

Dearer than eye-sight, space, and liberty;
Beyond what can be valued, rich or rare;
No less than life, with grace, health, beauty, honour;
As much as child e'er loved, or father found;
A love that makes breath poor, and speech unable;
Beyond all manner of so much I love you.

Joy

Very good. Yes.
(*Drops character, to* **Liam**.)
Off book for tomorrow, yes?
(*Back in character.*)
Yes yes yes indeed. Have some land. Land for Goneril,
there ya go.
What says our second daughter,
Our dearest Regan? Speak.

Liam *switches dresses.*

Liam

Sir, I am made
Of the self-same metal that my sister is,
And prize me at her worth. In my true heart
I find she names my very deed of love;
Only she comes too short: that I profess
Myself an enemy to all other joys,
Which the most precious square of sense possesses;
And find I am alone felicitate
In your dear highness' love.

Joy

Excellent! Very good Regan.
There you go – nice bit of kingdom for you.
Landlandland.
Now! Our joy
Cordelia, the youngest,
What can you say to draw a third more opulent than your
sisters?

Joy *does this bit on her own, swapping between dress and crown with crew's help.*

Joy (*as Cordelia*)
Nothing.

Joy (*as Lear*)
Nothing?

Joy (*as Cordelia*)
Nothing, my lord.

Joy (*as Lear*)
Well nothing will come of nothing! Speak again.

Joy (*as Cordelia*)
Unhappy that I am, I cannot heave
My heart into my mouth. I love you
According to my bond, no more nor less.

Joy (*as Lear*)
Thy heart goes with this?

Joy (*as Cordelia*)
Yes.

Joy (*as Lear*)
So young and so untender?
Let it be so; Thy truth then be thy dower
Here I disclaim all my paternal care,
(*Getting angry. Getting into it. Fumbling for the threads of it.*)
Here I disclaim my paternal care!
Here I disclaim all my *parental* care!
Here I disclaim all my parental care
You are a stranger to my heart and me
A stranger!
(*She has it now.*)
For, by the sacred radiance of the sun,
The mysteries of Hecate, and the night;
By all the operation of the orbs
From whom we do exist, and cease to be;
Here I disclaim all my paternal care . . .

And property . . . and blood . . .
And blah and blah
As thou my sometime daughter.
(*Suddenly to* **Conor**.) Peace, Kent!
Come not between the dragon and his wrath.
I loved her most,
and thought that she would nurse me
I loved her most
And thought that she would be my nurse
(*To the Cordelia dress.*)
I loved you the most
I loved you the most
I was to give you the most beautiful part of the kingdom,
where the mountains meet the sea, where you could build
a little cottage on your land and I could come and visit
you. And give little performances from the repertoire.
And have your children implore me to tell stories of my
kingly career. 'Pappy, pappy, pappy!' They'd say. 'Tell us
how great you are.' Well, it's clear to me now that I was
blinded by my love for you. I see you for who you really
are now. Get thee gone!

Joy *weeps for a long time.* **Joy** *suddenly drops character.*

Joy

Ok. Moving on?

Music out. LX change. Little round of applause. Crew resetting.

Joy

It wasn't too much was it?

Liam

That was great I thought. (*To* **Conor**, *bringing him in.*)
What did you think?

Joy

I just went with it. I think it could go bigger still, what do
you think?

Liam
Maybe yeah, yeah.

Joy
I think so.

Liam (*to* **Conor**)
You'd agree, would you?

Joy
Who is this?

Liam
Oh Joy, this is . . . (*Leaving a slight pause for* **Joy** *to fill.*)

Joy
. . . oh, the understudy!

Liam
Yes! The understudy!

Joy
Right well . . . nice to meet you. Try to keep up. Hahaha!
(*To the room.*) Are we there? Ok and . . .

Let Me Not Be Mad

Back in the performance. **Joy** *is in character as Lear. Outside the palace.* **Liam** *is off book for this and the Fool scenes in general.* **Conor** *is awkward in the background.*

Joy
Fool! Fool! Where is my Fool?

Liam
Here nuncle! Always here.

Joy
Fool! Did you see? Her monster ingratitude?
Well I showed her.
Gave her nothing because if that's all I am to her, that's all she is to me

Ha!

(*To* **Cordelia** *off stage.*)

You'll regret the day you failed to fill my heart with love!
Get out of my life!

Back to **Liam**. *Silence. She's less sure of her decision now.* **Liam**
knows it.

Liam

Thou canst tell why one's nose stands i'
the middle on's face?

Joy

No.

Liam

Why, to keep one's eyes of either side's nose; that
what a man cannot smell out, he may spy into.

Joy

I did her wrong.

Liam

Canst tell how an oyster makes his shell?

Joy

No.

Liam

Nor I neither; but I can tell why a snail has a house.

Joy

Why?

Liam

Why, to put his head in; not to give it away to his
daughters, and leave his horns without a case.

Joy

I will forget my nature. So kind a father! Be my
horses ready?

Liam

Thy asses are gone about 'em. The reason why the
seven stars are no more than seven is a pretty reason.

Joy

Because they are not eight?

Liam

Thou wouldst make a good Fool, nuncle!

Joy

Yeah?

Liam

Yeah. And if you were my Fool, I'd have you beaten for
being old before thy time.
Thou shouldst not have been old till thou hadst been wise.

Joy *is scared.* **Joy** *puts her forehead to* **Liam***'s.*

Joy

O, let me not be mad
not mad, sweet heaven
Keep me in temper: I would not be mad!

Liam

Shhhhhhhhhhh . . . there there . . .

A moment of stillness.

Joy *calms and wants to move on. She claps at a crew member to
turn the music on.*

Bender

*Music starts. Crew gives her a mic and water bottle. She downs the
water.* **Conor** *is awkward in the background.*

Joy (*spoken*) And the King never thought about his youngest
daughter again.

He went to live in Goneril's house with his group of one hundred favourite knights and his trusted Fool.
And never thought about his youngest daughter again.

(*Sung.*)
We are having a good time
A daughter is dead to me
Death of me she'll be
But we're having a good time

(*Spoken.*) And each day he and his knights went out hunting delicious dear and wild pigs and little darling wrens.

And he never thought about his youngest daughter again.

And each evening he and his knights would drink and feast and fuck. And drink and feast and fuck. And drink and feast and fuck. And drink. And feast. And fuck.

And he never thought about his youngest daughter again.

(*Sung*)
We are having a good time
A daughter is dead to me
Death of me she'll be
But we're having a good time

(*Spoken.*) And each full moon, he and his hundred knights would go into the city and go carousing in the city's pleasure dens.

(*Chanting, getting others going.*)
   And drinking and feasting and fucking
   And drinking and feasting and fucking
   And drinking and feasting and fucking

(*Feeling faint from the exertion.*) And he never, and he never, and never . . .

Tired now, still trying to party, but the fire is dying.

Liam *comes in with a chair. She sits.*

Liam

Did ya have a good time?

Hangover

A sitting room in the palace. **Joy** *is hungover, sitting in the chair.*
Liam *puts a costume shawl over her shoulders.*

Joy

No the other one!

He gets it. Puts it on. It feels better.

Joy

Servant! Servant! Servant!
(*No one will serve her. To Fool.*)
Fool, I have noticed we are not entertained with that
ceremonious affection as we are wont.

Liam

I have perceived a most faint neglect of late.

Joy

I think there's a great abatement of kindness here. Go and
get my daughter! I want a word. Does she not know who I
am?

Liam *goes to change costume.*

Liam

You're King Lear!

Joy

Too right I'm King Lear.

Liam *vamps while getting into costume.*

Liam

Goneril! Your father would like a word with you.

Joy

Come on Goneril!

Liam
He's in his comfy chair!

Liam *gets into position.*

Liam (*as Goneril*)
What?

Joy
There you are! I was just saying I have noticed we are not entertained with that ceremonious affection as we are wont. There's a great abatement of kindness here. And I think you and your people need to address it.

Liam (*reading*)
Not only, sir, this your all-licensed fool,
But other of your insolent retinue
Do hourly carp . . .

Joy
Oh you don't have to do all the lines. Just play the intention, play the *intention*.

Liam (*drops script, improvises*)
Right. Eh. Ok. Your pals . . . eh your friends . . . they're ruining my house . . . and it's *my* house . . . and they're ruining it. You're ruining it.
You're pigs.
You're brutes.
You and your knights, you terrify the children.
You've all your money spent on scratch cards.
You bore the servants to tears with your endless stories of the old days.
You sniff my handmaidens' underwear.
You've been heating and eating and reheating the same tub of soup for weeks.
The attic conversion that I got done quite recently . . . they got all sick in it.
And I won't stand for it any longer.
You're going to have to send some of them away.

One hundred knights! That number is way too high!
At least half will have to go.

Joy

Half? Of my knights?

Liam

At least half yes. At least. Leaving you with fifty. If not
twenty. Five. One. Why not?

Joy

But which half? You try and choose between one half of
your best knights and the other!

Liam

But what do you need them for? There's plenty of servants
here to look after you?

Joy

O reason not the need!
I gave you all!
But kept a reservation to be followed
You said I could live here with my hundred knights and
that's all there is to it!
Actually, you know what?
Never mind.
I have another daughter!
Regan!

Liam

Regan! Dad would like a word. He's in a pisser!

Liam *goes to change costume but stops when he sees* **Conor**. *He has
an idea. Indicates to the crew to give* **Conor** *the costume instead.*
Conor *is not happy about this.* **Liam** *vamps while* **Conor** *is
costumed.*

Liam

Regan. Regan, Dad would like a word. He's by the fire!

Joy

Oh come on Regan!

Liam *finds the right page for him and shows him where to stand.*

Conor (*as Regan, not good at it*)
Whereto our health is bound; we are not ourselves, when
nature, being oppressed, commands the mind,
To suffer with the body.
Sir, you are old.
Nature in you stands on the very verge
Of her confine: you should be ruled and led
By some discretion, that discerns your state
Better than you yourself

Joy (*dropping character*)
Are you going to do it that way? You're killing it. Here.
(*As Regan, sweet, patronising.*)
Dad, King, Your Majesty, I *really* think you should listen to
us when we tell you that you're a total fucking mess, ok?
You've been wearing the same clothes since you got here. I
know we said we wouldn't put you in a home but, to be
fucking honest with you, it suits me better to go back on
that. Ya know? You're smart enough to know what's going
on here. So, let's look at *all the options* . . . all the options *we*
propose. Ok?
(*As Lear.*)
Doth any here know me? This is not Lear:
Doth Lear walk thus? speak thus? Where are his eyes?
Who is it that can tell me who I am?
Who is it that can tell me who I am?
Who is it that can tell me who I am?
I gave you all!
Made you guardians, my depositaries;
I gave you all!
But kept a reservation to be followed
I will have such revenge on you both
That all the world shall – I will do such things –
What they are yet I know not; but they shall be
The terrors of the earth.
(*To* **Conor**.) May you have children!
May you have horrible ungrateful children.

May they turn all their mother's pains and benefits
To laughter and contempt; that you may feel
How sharper than a serpent's tooth it is
To have a thankless child!

Conor *needs to get out. Walks quickly downstage and out of the room.*

Liam and Conor I

Curtain draws across the downstage. **Conor** *is outside* **Joy**'s *room on his own.*

Conor

Fuck fuck fuck fuck fuck fuck fuck fuck fuck fuck fuck fuck fuck.

Liam *gently enters.*

Liam

How ya doing there Conor?

Conor

Fuck! Sorry. Yeah good yeah. Fuck. Sorry.

Liam

A bit overwhelming I'd say.

Conor

Yeah. A bit yeah. (*Pause.*) It's just . . . I don't know how to . . . do this . . .

Liam

Ok . . .

Conor

I don't know what role to take or whatever and I feel like a spare . . . I was never really anywhere near this part of her life.

Liam

I hear you.

Conor

I mean, I went to see her sometimes. Opening nights and that. When I'd be up in Dublin.

Liam

Oh?

Conor

I hated it to be honest. I never knew what to say to her afterwards. I hated it.

Liam

Ahh.

Conor

So this probably isn't the best way in for me . . . I know this is what you've been working with so far and it's *great* . . . but like maybe we could start to look at something else at some stage. I found these letters when I was clearing out her house . . . maybe we could . . . maybe we could . . .

Liam

See, we don't choose the Memory Theme, it comes from the person themselves.

Conor

Right.

Liam

Yeah.

Conor

It's just you *seem* to be . . . I mean you say 'shall we take a look at this?' and then she starts . . .

Liam

That came from lots and lots of trial and error.

Conor

Right.

Liam

And listening.

Conor

Right.

Liam

Which we started from early on.

Conor

Ok.

Liam

That only works as a prompt because she wants it to. We just kept listening and listening, and trying different things . . .

Conor

Yeah.

Liam

What you're not seeing is all the prompts and themes that didn't work . . .

Conor

Gotcha, gotcha.

Liam

Before we got to this one.

Conor

Got it. Ok.

Pause. **Conor** *is distracted.*

Liam

Did you . . . ever see this one? Her as King Lear?

Conor

Hmmm? No. No.

Liam

No, of course! Sorry. You would only been . . .? Would you have even been born?

Conor

I was one.

Liam

Ah. Must have really been something! For its time, like.

Conor

Yeah. I mean . . . I don't know. She kept on doing lines from plays when she got sick. I tried to get her to stop. Tell her it wasn't real. But I suppose that wasn't the right thing to do . . .

Pause.

Liam

Come on, we'll go in again. This next bit's a bit of fun.

Curtain draws back.

Storm

In the rehearsal room. **Joy**. *Crew. Preparation.*

Liam

Ok Joy, shall we have a look at this?

Joy *into position.*

Joy

This heart
Shall break into a hundred thousand flaws
Or ere I'll weep!

Joy *stops. Drops character. Something's wrong. The storm effects haven't gone off.*

Joy

What the fuck? Are we not all ready?

Liam

Sorry Joy! Late on the cue there. We'll take it from your line again.

Joy

This heart
Shall break into a hundred thousand flaws
Or ere I'll weep!

Storm sound, visuals, lightning, blowing wind from fans to match her anger. This is the most 'complete' the production has been.

Joy

Blow, winds, and crack your cheeks! rage! blow!
You cataracts and hurricanes, spout
Till you have drench'd our steeples, drown'd the cocks!
Thunderbolts!
Singe my white head!
Crack nature's moulds!
I'm going
I'm going out
Into the storm
To feel my feelings!
(*Intimate, to herself.*)
Let me not be mad, not mad
Not mad o
Let me not be mad please not mad
(*To the landscape.*)
Rumble thy bellyful! Spit, fire! spout, rain!
Nor rain, wind, thunder, fire, are my daughters:
I tax not you, you elements, with unkindness;
I never gave you kingdom, call'd you children,
(*Looking around.*)
Fool! Fool! Where is my Fool?

Liam

O nuncle, court holy-water in a dry
house is better than this rain-water out o' door.
Good nuncle, in, and ask thy daughters' blessing:
here's a night pities neither wise man nor fool.

Joy (*to the landscape*)

Singe my white head! And thou, all-shaking thunder,
Smite flat the thick rotundity o' the world!
Crack nature's moulds, an germens spill at once,
That make ingrateful man!
(*Losing it.*)
Ingrateful man

Ingrateful, ingrateful
ingrateful, man
(*Intimate, to herself.*)
Let me not be mad, not mad
Not mad o
Let me not be mad please not mad
I am a poor, infirm, weak, and despised old man:
(*To the landscape.*)
Cordelia! Cordelia! Where are you?
My wits begin to turn.
Come on, my boy: how dost, my boy?

Conor
Yes! Yes! I'm here, Mum. Mum?

Storm effects suddenly gone. Illusion broken.

Conor
Dad . . . Your majesty?

Joy *looks at* **Conor** *with suspicion.* **Liam** *and crew watch* **Joy** *for her reaction.* **Joy** *moves on.*

Reconciliation

Joy
Fool!

Liam
Here nuncle. Always here.

Joy
A sovereign shame so elbows me. Cordelia. Go and get her. I need to speak to her.

Liam *and crew now know where they are. A pleasant meadow. Crew put on nice music.* **Joy** *plays Cordelia very sweetly.*

Joy (*as Cordelia*)
O you kind gods,
Cure this great breach in his abused nature!

The untuned and jarring senses, O, wind up
Of this child-changed father!

Liam (*as Doctor*)
So please your majesty
That we may wake the King: he hath slept long.

Joy (*as Cordelia*)
Is he array'd?

Liam (*as Gentleman*)
Ay, madam; in the heaviness of his sleep
We put fresh garments on him.

Joy (*as Cordelia*)
O my dear father! Restoration hang
Thy medicine on my lips; and let this kiss
Repair those violent harms that my two sisters
Have in thy reverence made!
Alack, alack!
'Tis wonder that thy life and wits at once
Had not concluded all. He wakes; speak to him.

Liam (*as Doctor*)
Madam, do you; 'tis fittest.

Joy (*as Cordelia*)
How does my royal lord? How fares your majesty?

Liam *puts the crown of flowers on* **Joy**'s *head when she's Lear and takes it off when she's Cordelia. He holds the crown in position where Lear's head was in order to give* **Joy** *an eyeline.*

Joy (*as Lear*)
You do me wrong to take me out o' the grave:
Thou art a soul in bliss; but I am bound
Upon a wheel of fire, that mine own tears
Do scald like molten lead.

Joy (*as Cordelia*)
Sir, do you know me?

Liam *gestures to* **Conor** *to take his place; holding the crown and taking it off as* **Liam** *has been doing.* **Joy** *doesn't seem to notice.*

Joy (*as Lear*)
Pray, do not mock me:
I am a very foolish fond old man,
Methinks I should know you,
Yet I am doubtful for I am mainly ignorant
Where I did lodge last night. Do not laugh at me;
For, as I am a man, I think this lady
To be my child Cordelia.

Joy (*as Cordelia*)
And so I am, I am.

Joy (*as Lear*)
Be your tears wet? yes, 'faith. I pray, weep not:
If you have poison for me, I will drink it.
I know you do not love me; for your sisters
Have, as I do remember, done me wrong:
You have some cause, they have not.

Joy (*as Cordelia*)
No cause, no cause.

Joy (*as Lear*)
Pray you now, forget and forgive:
I am old and foolish.

Joy (*as Cordelia*)
Of course I will Dad. All is forgiven
(*To the room.*)
And it was. Curtain!

Applause.

Joy
It's coming. It's coming . . . (*about the flower crown*) I'm not sure about this though . . . feels a little undercooked.

Liam

Oh? Clodagh, would you mind having a word with Joy? She has some notes about the crown.

Fussing and resetting. **Liam** *leaves the room. Curtain draws.*

Liam and Conor II

Downstage of the curtain. **Liam** *is at the nurse's station.* **Conor** *steps out of* **Joy***'s room into this corridor.* **Liam** *doesn't notice him.* **Conor** *is about to go but wants to linger.*

Conor

Thanks Liam.

Liam

Thank you Conor.

Conor

She'll be ok in there without us?

Liam

Yeah, she'll do notes with Clodagh for a bit and then she might go again at some point.

Conor

Right. You're very good with her.

Liam

Ah thanks.

Conor

No you are. You're really good. She likes you. And she doesn't like most people.

Liam

Ha! Well I'm very fond of her too.

Conor

And the lines and everything. You've them nearly learned off.

Liam

Thanks! I actually know more than I let on at this stage. But then I realised she actually likes to give out to me. So now I just pretend I'm reading them.

Conor

She does like to give out! No, you're very good with her.

Liam

Ah, I like it! I was into the drama a bit when I was in college. More musicals and that than Shakespeare but . . .

Conor

Oh really?

Liam

Haven't had the chance to do much of it since.

Conor

And the other residents . . . were they also actors or . . .?

Liam

Huh? Oh. No, there's all sorts of people here.

Conor

And do they all just think they're at their jobs?

Liam

Not necessarily their jobs, though sometimes it is. Your Memory Theme is usually something that you were good at. Something that gives you a sense of self-esteem. (*Pause.*) Did you ever do a bit of acting or anything?

Conor

No.

Liam

Follow in the mammy's footsteps?

Conor

God no. No no no no no. (*Pause.*) Ok well . . . see you tomorrow Liam.

Liam

Take care Conor.

Conor

Same time?

Liam

Whatever suits.

Conor *goes to go but turns back.*

Conor

Liam, is this working? For her?

Liam

It is, yes. All things considered this is a good situation. I know it might seem peculiar, from your point of view . . .

Conor

Peculiar? Yeah.

Liam

. . . coming in at quite a late point, I mean usually the family would be involved . . .

Conor

I mean I've had a lot on.

Liam

Of course! It's just normally you'd have seen all the steps to get here . . .

Conor

Sure it's just . . .

Liam

I understand completely . . .

Conor

We weren't very close. Aren't very close.

Liam

It must be very shocking, seeing it all at once.

Conor

Yeah it is yeah.

Liam

I understand. I do. (*Pause.*) She can't have been an easy person to grow up with.

Conor

Well I didn't grow up with her. But yeah no. She was difficult. Even before all this.

Liam

But you can see it, I hope. She's content. She's empowered.

Conor

Empowered?

Liam

It's such a disempowering disease. Anything we can do to help Joy feel like she's in control, like she still has status, is a good thing.

Conor

Look. I just want to talk to her normally, like. I want to . . . to bring the kids in . . . and myself, like, I want to be able to . . . I found these letters in her room . . . I want to be able to talk to her without all this . . . getting in the way.

Liam

You *can* do that of course.

Conor

I can?

Liam

You can, yes. Your mother's care is entirely up to you, at this stage. But . . .

Conor

But?

Liam

Well you've *seen* what it's like when you try to force her into accepting *your* reality . . .

Conor

Right.

Liam

She doesn't understand . . .

Conor

Yeah.

Liam

. . . worse than that, it makes her *very* distressed.

Conor

Got it yeah.

Liam

So we'd advise, as I said, that you *go* with whatever her reality is. That's the best, I would say, *only* way to be in her company at this stage. Avoid asking her direct questions. Don't say 'hello' or 'good morning' because she might not have experienced time passing in the way that you did. Just . . . listen. React. Let her tell you where she wants to be. If you try and tell her where you think she is . . . well, you saw what happened earlier when you . . .

Conor

Yes. Yes I saw that. Thanks Liam. (*Pause.*) And so, what? You'd just say; it's all about her now? It's all about what she needs? And anyone . . . who wants to meet her . . . anyone else's needs . . . they just have to be in *her* world?

Liam

Well, yes . . . be in her world. That's the disease. (*Pause.*) She'll find a role for you in this. You'll see. But on her terms.

Conor *exits. Curtain draws and we are in a new day.*

Act II

Liam *enters. Crew. Preparation.*

Liam
Getting there!

Joy
Mmm . . . yes, getting there getting there. Though we're
going to have to pick up the pace a bit I think.

Liam
Oh?

Joy
Yes you need to pick up your cues more. It's getting a
bit . . .

Conor *enters.*

Conor (*interrupting*)
Morning, Joy. Morning, Liam.

Joy *is frozen, looking at him.*

Conor
I mean . . . sorry. Hello. No. I mean, fuck. I'm not
supposed to. Sorry. Not 'Hello' just 'hi, I'm here'. Fuck . . .
Sorry Liam.

Liam (*deflecting*)
Alright Joy, shall we have a look at this?

Joy
Yes let's. Let's do act four, scene seven.

Liam
Right so, Joy.

Liam *gives a thumbs up to* **Conor** *– this is good. Preparing. They
put* **Conor** *in Cordelia's dress and give him a script.*

Liam (*to* **Conor**)
Ay, madam; in the heaviness of his sleep
We put fresh garments on him.

Conor
O . . .

Joy *interrupts and takes over as Cordelia.* **Liam** *encourages*
Conor *to stick at it.*

Joy (*Cordelia*)
O my dear father! Restoration hang
Thy medicine on my lips; and let this kiss
Repair those violent harms that my two sisters
Have in thy reverence made!
Alack, alack!
'Tis wonder that thy life and wits at once
Had not concluded all. He wakes; speak to him.

Liam (*to* **Conor**)
Madam, do you; 'tis fittest.

Conor
How . . .

Joy *interrupts again and does a very fast, perfunctory version of*
this scene.

Joy (*as Cordelia*)
How does my royal lord? How fares your majesty?

Joy (*as Lear*)
You do me wrong to take me out o' the grave:
Thou art a soul in bliss; but I am bound
Upon a wheel of fire, that mine own tears
Do scald like molten lead.

Joy (*as Cordelia*)
Sir, do you know me?

Crew try to put the flower crown on **Joy** *but she bats it away*
without stopping.

Joy (*as Lear*)
   Pray, do not mock me:
   I am a very foolish fond old man,
   Methinks I should know you,
   Yet I am doubtful for I am mainly ignorant
   Where I did lodge last night. Do not laugh at me;
   For, as I am a man, I think this lady
   To be my child Cordelia.

Joy (*as Cordelia*)
   And so I am, I am.

Joy (*as Lear*)
   Be your tears wet? yes, 'faith. I pray, weep not:
   If you have poison for me, I will drink it.
   I know you do not love me; for your sisters
   Have, as I do remember, done me wrong:
   You have some cause, they have not.

Joy (*as Cordelia*)
   No cause, no cause.

Joy (*as Lear*)
   Pray you now, forget and forgive:
   I am old and foolish.

Joy (*as Cordelia*)
   Of course I will Dad. All is forgiven
   (*To the room.*)
   And it was. Curtain!

Applause. **Joy** *retires to her chair.*

Joy
   Well, what did we think?

Conor
   I thought that was good, Joy. I thought that was great.

Liam
   Great!

Conor

Could I try?

Joy

Who is this?

Liam

Oh Joy this is . . . .

Joy

Oh the understudy.

Liam

Yes, we're rehearsing in the understudies today.

Conor

Please.

Liam

I think we should. No? While we have the understudy
here we should rehearse them in.

Joy

Is he off book?

Liam

He's not off book yet but . . .

Conor

Please. I'm still learning the lines but I'd like to give it a go.

Joy

Oh alright let's see where we are with it.

She gets into position. Crew help **Conor** *back into the dress.* **Liam**
helps him with the scipt.

Conor (*reading*)

O you kind gods,
Cure this great breach in his abused nature!
The untuned and jarring senses, O, wind up

Joy (*pronouncing it correctly*)

Wind!

Conor
> Wind up
> Of this child-changed father!

Liam
> So please your majesty
> That we may wake the King: he hath slept long.

Conor
> Is he arid?

Joy
> Array'd!

Conor
> Arraay'd.

Liam
> Ay, madam; in the heaviness of his sleep
> We put fresh garments on him.

Conor
> O my dear father! Restoration hang
> Thy medicine on my lips; and let this kiss . . .

Joy (*sitting up*)
> Oh Liam, I can't bear this. He's breaking up the lines!

Liam
> Maybe just let him finish this small bit. You'll come in now
> in a sec.

Joy (*lying back down*)
> Fine.

Conor
> Repair those violent harms that my two sisters
> Have in thy reverence made!
> Alack, alack!
> 'Tis wonder that thy life and wits at once
> Had not concluded all. He wakes; speak to him.

Liam

Madam, do you; 'tis fittest.

Conor

How does my royal lord? How fares your majesty?

Joy *never looks at* **Conor**.

Joy (*as Lear*)

You do me wrong to take me out o' the grave:
Blah Blah Blah Blah Blah.

She skips ahead. **Conor** *looks for help from* **Liam**. *Finds it in the script for him.*

Joy

Be your tears wet? yes, 'faith. I pray, weep not:
If you have poison for me, I will drink it.
I know you do not love me; for your sisters
Have, as I do remember, done me wrong:
You have some cause, they have not.

Conor

No cause, no cause.

Joy

Pray you now, forget and forgive:
I am old and foolish.
And all was forgiven Curtain!

Conor *turns over the page, looking for where he got lost.*
Applause.

Joy

Pretty good, pretty good. You'll be fine when you're off book.

Liam

Great, Joy, well done. We'll be glad of that extra bit of work now.

Joy

We will, we will.

Liam

Tea?

Joy

Please.

Conor (*interrupting*)

Could we go again? Please. I'd like to do it again.

Joy

Again?

Conor

Yeah I'd like another go at it. You know the way Liam does it sometimes, where he says things that aren't exactly . . . that aren't in the play.

Liam

You want to 'play the intention'?

Conor

Yeah that!

Joy

Well that's specific to Liam . . . he can do that.

Conor

Please. I'd like a go of it. I'll be quick.

Liam

Maybe no harm Joy? Show the young lad.

Joy

He's not a young lad, he's a middle-aged man.

Liam

Ah I know but he's new. He could do with being shown how things are done here. What dya think? One more?

Joy

Oh alright. We'll go from when Lear wakes.

Quick preparation. **Conor** *is gentle and present and seeking her eye with his questions. It unsettles her.*

Conor

Hi. Dad. King. Hi.

Joy

You do me wrong to take me out o' the grave:
Thou art a soul in bliss; but I am bound
Upon a wheel of fire, that mine own tears
Do scald like molten lead.

Conor *goes down to her and puts himself in her eyeline.*

Conor

Do you recognise me?

Joy *is unsettled.*

Joy

You are a spirit, I know: when did you die?
Where have I been? Where am I? Fair daylight?
I am mightily abused.

Conor

Look. It's me. Me. Your daughter. Cordelia?

Joy

Let's stop this there! No, no, no it won't do.

Conor

It's Cordelia, Dad! I got your letters. Your letters . . . that's
why I'm here.

Joy

No no no no this is all wrong.

Liam

Righto Joy. Time for our break anyway.

Crew shuffle **Conor** *away. Dress is taken off.* **Joy** *sits in her seat.*

Liam (*to* **Conor***, for* **Joy***'s benefit*)

Good, good. We'll leave it there. Learn those lines.

Liam *tries to restore* **Joy***'s confidence by engaging in some chat.*
Conor *is thinking.*

Joy

I mean we've tried, and it doesn't work. He either learns the lines or . . .

Conor (*interrupting*)

Yeah so I thought it was interesting . . . I thought it was interesting the way she forgives him.

Joy *avoids* **Conor**'s *eye.*

Joy

Interesting?

Conor

Yeah. Yeah. Just making an observation there. It seems a bit of a stretch, don't you think?

Liam

Hahaha! I'd love to get mister Shakespeare on the phone and ask him about that.

Conor

Well it's just . . . Liam has been telling me about it, the play. I don't know it that well. I don't know it. It's very famous, obviously. Very well thought of. So I thought you might, Joy, have some . . . insight into why she, Cordelia, forgives Lear.

Joy

I mean who can say why anyone does anything?

Conor

Try.

Joy

Well . . . what did he do?

Conor

He kicked her out. She had to go to France. He was cruel, really horrible to her.

Joy

She forgives him because he's a foolish fond old man.
What else would she do?

Conor

Well ok but maybe he could say he's sorry.

Joy

He does.

Conor

No he doesn't, he says 'forget and forgive', that's not the
same thing.

Joy

That's good enough for her.

Conor

But it's not. It can't be.

Joy

Well . . . then . . . she shouldn't have a king for a father.

Pause.

Conor

I just don't buy it.

Long pause. **Joy** *sits with her feelings.*

Joy

Right. Liam. Shall we take a look at this? You (*to* **Conor**) be
Cordelia.

A bit of a frenzy trying to prepare. Putting **Conor** *in the dress.*
Putting things in position for the top of the show.

Joy

I've made my decision.
After many battles, and banquets, and trade wars, and
alliances, and traitors hung, and popes denounced, and
awards won, and ships built, and lands discovered, and
monasteries sacked, and sun rises toasted . . .
I will make you my guardians, my depositories
But you have to love me.

You have to love me
You have to say you love me
There's money in it for you. There's land. Some marshy
bits and some coastal bits. Some bits with woods in them.
Some wheat fields. Some nice houses and a boat.
I'll give it all to you if you say you'll love me and that you'll
look after me.
You have to look at me now and tell me I'm good, that this
is good . . .
That the bits of you that I can't see are changed, charged,
churned by the bits of me that you can't see
Right Goneril, our first born. What says you?

Liam *steps up dressed as Goneril.*

Joy (*before he's had a chance*)
Very good! Very good! Well done Goneril.
And now, Regan. The middle child. What now from you?
Regan goes *blah blah blah*
I go 'fine'. Fine, I don't believe you but fine.
Now, our joy!
What can you say to draw a third more opulent than your
sisters?

She turns her ferocity on **Conor** *as Cordelia.*

Conor
Nothing.

Joy
Nothing?

Conor
Nothing, my lord.

Joy
Well nothing will come of fucking nothing! Speak again.

Conor (*reading*)
Unhappy that I am, I cannot heave
My heart into my mouth: I love you
According to my bond; no more nor less.

Joy

Give it some fucking umph can't you?

Conor

Unhappy that I am . . .

Joy

Come on.

Conor

Unhappy that I am . . .

Joy

Come on!

Conor

I cannot heave, my heart into my mouth.

Joy

Your heart? What fucking heart? You think you're worthy of a king's inheritance?

Conor

I love you.

Joy

Speak up!

Conor

I love you. I love you according to my bond.

Joy

I don't believe you! Liam! Fool!

Liam

Yes nuncle, always here.

Joy

Oh don't call me nuncle. I've completely dropped character now. I don't know where I am. We'll have to get someone else in for . . . How am I to be expected to play opposite that? How is anyone supposed to believe in him?

Conor *takes the dress off. Dejected.*

Liam

Yes Joy, you're absolutely right. Don't know what I was thinking.

Joy

I don't remember him auditioning. Is that really who we went with?

Liam

He's actually just understudying today, but we're due our break now anyway.

Conor

Oh for god's sake Liam this is fucking madness.

Conor *approaches* **Joy** *directly.*

Conor

Mum. It's me! Conor. I'm Conor. Your son. I'm here to speak to you. You. Not this nonsense. I've just come to say . . . I've come to speak to you . . .

Sudden change in atmosphere. The air has been sucked out of the room.

Joy

Conor? No.

Joy *looks at herself in the mirror and sees an old woman.*

Light and sound – a horrible lurching sensation.

Act III

The Calm Before The Storm

Curtain draws across the downstage dividing **Joy** *from the rest of the stage, her old face disappears. As if waking from a nightmare into an in-between space.*

Joy
 Liam! Fool!

Liam *enters as Fool.*

Liam
 Shall we take a look at this?

Joy
 No! No, I think we're due our break now anyway.

Liam
 Right you are.

Joy
 I thought I'd lost track there . . .

Liam
 Oh?

Joy
 Yes, but I have it now.

Liam
 You now have what you lost?

Joy
 Yes.

Liam
 Which is 'track'?

Joy
 Yes.

Liam
Well that must make you very at*trac*tive.

Joy (*ignoring that*)
There's nothing quite as terrifying, for an actor, as drying.

Liam
No fear of that in the storm scene though, hah?

Joy (*ignoring that*)
It's so completely exposing. Everything you've been doing to get them to believe in the illusion, all the work, all the frothing something out of nothing . . . all evaporates in a moment. Dry. You're not Lear. You're just some woman in a crown. You're dead matter. Particles. Conspiring into the shape of a king, but actually now . . . you're just in the shape of a fucking fool.

Liam
None taken.

Joy
In those moments of dry you forget who you are. Where you are. Nothing but a terrifying blank. I'm nothing. I'm dead.

Liam
You are nothing, but you're not dead.

Joy
How is that? Surely if I'm nothing it's the same as being dead.

Liam
Close your eyes. Put your fingers in there.

Liam *hands her a box of envelopes.*

Liam
What do you feel?

Joy
Envelopes. It's a box of envelopes.

Liam

Squeeze.

Joy

Ah now I feel it. You've put a little stone or a hard ball in there. Like a marble. But you've suspended it somehow in the middle of the box. How have you done that?

She starts taking the envelopes out of the box looking for the marble.

Joy

Where is it? What is this?

Liam

There is no marble. Or rather, there is, it's just not in that box. The paper folds and overlaps in the centre of each envelope, creating an area that's slightly thicker than the rest. Repeat that over and over for hundreds of envelopes and squeeze. The impression is unmistakable.

Joy

It's as real to me as anything I've felt and yet . . .

Liam

When you take it apart, where does it go? The marble's existence is dependent on the confluence of many tiny, otherwise independent physical events which, in themselves are nothing, but when pressed together are what we call something.

Lightning, like firing synapses.

Liam

Each time you touched cold (*showing an envelope*), tasted sweet (*another envelope*), saw your reflection (*another envelope*); each sensory experience you've had to date, created a pattern of electrical activity in your brain. The next time you saw your reflection, that pattern again. (*Puts an envelope in the box.*) And again (*another envelope*) and again (*another envelope*). We call those electrical patterns that we return to, 'memories'. They're the tiny folds of paper, increasing the thickness of the envelope by one iota at a time. Press enough of them together, add enough energy, and you get a marble. You get you. That pressure, that storm that makes you, is blowing out and taking the envelopes with it. So when you dry, when you look for your line and find it's not where you put it, when you ask 'who is it that can tell me who I am?' and find only Lear's shadow, know that you are as you ever were. You're nothing. But you're not dead.

Joy

Peace, peace, Mercutio, peace!
Thou talk'st of nothing.

Thunder.

Liam

Hey ho, the wind and the rain!

Joy

Keep me on track, won't you? Keep me on track.

Liam (*speaking past her to someone unseen*)

There's nothing for it, I'm afraid . . .

Joy

Keep me on track.

Liam

. . . all we can do is manage it at this point . . .

Joy

Please.

Liam

. . . this is a good situation, all things considered.

Joy

· I don't want this, I don't want to blow out. I want to rage blow! The storm is the only thing that makes sense!

Liam *exits, sound shift, lighting change.*

The Storm (Part 1 – Rumbles)

An uncanny shift. The lighting comes slowly up behind the gauze curtain, and we see a reprise of the action from Act II. The setting is almost the exact same but it's now taking place in a nursing home. The crew are now carers. **Joy** *has been replaced by a puppet – a much more elderly version of herself. Downstage of the curtain the younger* **Joy** *voices the older* **Joy**.

Joy

Now, our joy!
What can you say to draw a third more opulent than your sisters?

Conor

Nothing.

Joy

Nothing?

Conor

Nothing, my lord.

Joy

Well nothing will come of fucking nothing! Speak again.

Conor (*reading*)

Unhappy that I am, I cannot heave
My heart into my mouth: I love you
According to my bond; no more nor less.

Joy

Give it some fucking umph can't you?

Conor

Unhappy that I am . . .

Joy

Come on.

Conor

Unhappy that I am . . .

Joy

Come on!

Conor

I cannot heave, my heart into my mouth.

Joy

Your heart? What fucking heart? You think you're worthy of a king's inheritance?

Conor

I love you.

Joy

Speak up!

Conor

I love you. I love you according to my bond.

Joy

I don't believe you! Liam! Fool!

Liam

Yes nuncle, always here.

Joy

Oh don't call me nuncle. I've completely dropped character now. I don't know where I am. We'll have to get someone else in for . . . How am I to be expected to play opposite that? How is anyone supposed to believe in him?

Conor *takes the dress off. Dejected.*

Liam

Yes Joy, you're absolutely right. Don't know what I was thinking.

Joy

I don't remember him auditioning. Is that really who we went with?

Liam

He's actually just understudying today, but we're due our break now anyway.

Conor

Oh for god's sake Liam this is fucking madness. Mum. It's
me! Conor. I'm Conor. Your son. I'm here to speak to you.
You. Not this nonsense. I've just come to say . . . I've come
to speak to you . . .

Joy

Conor? No.
Fool! Where is my Fool?

Liam

Conor, can we leave it there?

Conor

No Liam, no. I'm sorry but look. She's my mother, I'll
speak to her how I want.

Liam

Conor, she's just a sick old lady.

Conor

No. No she's not just that.

Conor into the Camera I

Conor *looks into the camera, it's* **Joy***'s POV, and speaks to her
directly. It's projected large on the downstage curtain.*

Conor

Mum. Joy. Look. (*Pause.*) I found these. I found them in
your wardrobe at home. Letters. From me. Dozens of
them. And I want to talk to you about them. I want to
reach you. And talk about them.

Joy (*gentle, quietly*)

No no no let me not be mad not mad not mad.

Conor

Look at this. It's the first one I sent you.

> *'Dear Joy. My name is Conor. I am your son. My dad has told me all about you. I just wanted to write to you to tell you that I am alive and that I live in Carlow. And I am fifteen . . . '*

That doesn't seem right, does it? I read this now and think . . . I was a kid!

Joy (*getting louder*)
No no no no!

Sudden shift. Upstage of the curtain goes dark. Video of **Conor** *is gone.*

Young Conor I

Joy *on her own downstage of curtain. She sees* **Conor** *in front of her. We hear young* **Conor** *but don't see him.*

Joy
Conor?

Conor
Hi Joy.

Joy
Look how handsome you turned out!

Conor
Thanks for meeting me.

Joy
Oh my pleasure! Can we get you something?

Conor
Can I get a coke?

Joy
Are you sure that's all you want?

Conor
Yeah that's all I want thanks.

Joy

Would you not like something to eat?

Conor

Oh no no no, that's ok.

Joy

You're sure?

Conor

Yes thanks.

Joy

He'll just have a coke. (*Pause.*) Conor my boy, I was simply delighted when I got your letter.

Conor

Oh yeah?

Joy

Yes, it's been too long that we've been apart.

Conor

You think so?

Joy

I do.

Conor

Well that's great. I mean, I thought so too. That's why I wrote to you.

Joy

And I'm glad you did.

Conor

Well there's so much I want to know about you.

Joy

Oh?

Conor

Yeah I mean I've seen you on TV loads of times.

Joy

Oh the tellie! A necessary evil.

Conor

And I read about you in the papers. Reviews of your plays.

Joy

Eugh, critics.

Conor

And I tell people that's my mum and they don't believe me.

Joy

Hahahaha well . . .

Conor

But I don't care.

Joy

Good for you.

Conor

To be honest, Dad didn't want me to write.

Joy

No? Well. Now that I have you here, I'm going to spoil you rotten.

Conor

Ha! Ok. That sounds good.

Sudden shift.

Old Joy and Conor I

*Light upstage of the curtain. They are in **Joy**'s house. Old **Joy** is sitting in her chair. **Conor** is distracted tidying, doing little jobs, etc.*

Joy

I've made a decision. I've made a decision
I'm perfectly capable of making my own decisions.

Conor

My King?

Joy

It's my decision.

Conor

My Lord?

Joy

I've made a decision. Nobody is going to tell me what I can and can't do.

Conor

Good my Lord, thy council is thine own.

Joy

Your sisters . . . they took my lands. They've taken my things, my money . . .

Conor

I know not of what you speak.

Joy

Well not your sisters, but Goneril anyway, your, your . . .

Conor

No sisters have I
Being but a lone and scarcely wanted child

Pause.

Joy

Well you'll want to be going soon.

Conor

I've just arrived, Joy.

Joy

Oh yes. Of course. Well, tea then?

Conor

No, I'm grand thanks. How are you getting on then, with the carers in to help? They're good aren't they?

Joy

Oh I don't know. I'm quite tired actually.

Conor

Oh?

Joy

Yes, I didn't sleep well last night. It's the adrenaline you
see. Being on stage. Nothing like it. All those people
watching, turning something into nothing. If they go with
it, if they apply enough pressure . . . well . . . masks can
become faces, a woman can be a king and stories can have
endings. Something out of nothing.

Conor

Right, I think you're a bit confused there but that's ok.
That might be a memory. But that's fine . . . Is there
anything I can do?

Joy

I'm perfectly fine.

Conor

Anything I can do to help? I got the cleaners in and sorted
out the fridge anyway.

Joy

No I'm . . .

Conor

And the mice and the bird in the attic, all that's done
now . . .

Joy

O well flown bird!

Conor

It's just I'm in Carlow most days, the kids and everything.
But they're good aren't they? The carers? Better than the
last ones anyway . . .

Joy

I don't need any help. I get along fine without you. I've always depended on the kindness of strangers.

Conor

Sure, sure, ok. But Mum, I'm here for you.

Joy

Eugh don't call me 'mum', it debases you.

Conor

Fine, Joy, your majesty.

Joy

Grow up for heaven's sake and face the world.

Conor

I will yeah.

Joy

It's chaos out there. All is storms. And your mother can't help you.

Conor

That's not right.

Joy

Well it's true.

Conor

Well if it is, I don't know, but I know it's not right.

Sudden shift.

Conor at the Door

Conor *steps into the light, he can be seen through the gauze.*

Conor

Hi Mum, hi we brought cake. You in there?

Joy

Who's 'we' darling?

Conor
I'm here with the kids? They're looking forward to meeting you.

Joy
I'm afraid I have plans this evening I have people coming over.

Conor
No Joy. That's us. That's us.

Joy
I'm about to get dressed and leave now, shortly.

Conor
No need. No need.

Joy
You really will have to excuse me, I'm late already.

Conor
No no Joy it's us you're . . . we're your plans for the evening. I rang a little while ago I said I'd come over with . . .

Joy
I don't think you did. I've been in rehearsals all day.

Conor
Ya haven't Mum, ya haven't . . .

Joy
We're coming up to previews . . . and anyway . . . I don't believe we've met.

Conor
It's Conor. Your son.

Joy
No. My son lives in France. I sent him to France.

Conor
Carlow, Mum, but look, you're just a bit confused.

Joy

How dare you? I am not confused.

Conor

Ya are ya are ya are.

Joy

You're speaking to me as if I'm some sort of child.

Conor

You should be ruled by some discretion befitting of your state.

Joy

Please I have to go. Please. Please just take your foot out of the door.

Conor

Just sit down I'll make a cup of tea.

Joy

I don't want tea. I'll call the police.

Conor

That's ok, that's ok. You've done that before. They know you.

Joy

Please take your foot out of my door I have to be going.

Conor

There's places I'd rather be too, Joy, there's places I'd rather be too.

Sudden shift.

Old Joy and Conor II

Light upstage of the curtain. **Joy**'s *house.* **Conor** *is sitting with Old* **Joy**.

Joy

I'm perfectly capable of making my own decisions.

Conor

I know, Joy.

Joy

I've made a decision.

Conor

I know, I know Mum.

Joy

I can make decisions and I've made my mind up.

Conor

Great, Mum. What is it?

Joy

I've put your sisters in command of my affairs and now . . .
you know . . . I . . . don't like what they've done. We had a
deal. You know I told them . . .

Conor

This is from a story Mum, I don't think this is real . . .

Joy

No I told them. I told them . . . you can have my money
but you have to love me.

Conor

This is a story.

Joy

I said specifically, tell me how you love me . . . and then
keep me. But now they're not . . . now I know they don't
love me. And they've taken my lands. And they're
throwing me out of the house. They're throwing me out of
the house.

Conor

No one is throwing you out.

Joy

That's what they said but I couldn't live like that. I just
don't understand why they would do that to me. We had a
deal.

Conor

No one is throwing you out, there's just me.

Joy

They should love me. They should love me.

Conor

No one is throwing you out. It's just me, I don't have any sisters, you don't have any daughters and I'm not going to throw . . .

Joy

They should love me.

Conor

I do . . .

Joy

They should say they love me.

Conor

I do Mum. I do . . .

Joy

They should say it.

Conor

I . . . love you.

Joy

I don't believe you.

Conor

I do, I do. You're my mother. Of course I love you. You're my mother and that's all there is to it.

Joy

Speak again.

Conor

That's all there is to it, Joy.

Joy

Speak again.

Conor

I won't. I said it. I said it, you want me to say it again?

Joy

Yes.

Conor

I cannot heave
My heart into my mouth: I love you
According to my bond; nor more nor less
And I won't throw you out of the house.

Joy

Thy truth then be thy dower . . .

Conor

Ok look . . .

Joy

By the sacred radiance of sun
The mysteries of Hecate and the night
(*Pause.*)
I think you should go

Conor

I've just arrived. I've just arrived. I'll make the tea.

Sudden shift.

Young Conor II

Joy *alone, downstage of the curtain. We hear but don't see Young*
Conor*.*

Joy

Tell me, what did you think of your mother's performance
tonight?

Conor

It was good yeah.

Joy

'Good yeah.' Come on mister letter writer, use your words!

Conor

I . . . I thought it was great.

Joy

Great?

Conor

Yeah great.

Joy

Well, good then.

Conor

I . . . I don't know what I'm supposed to say.

Joy

. . . Gloucester's boy let him believe he'd thrown himself off a cliff, and by some miracle, landed safely on the earth below.

Conor

Sorry. What?

Joy

Can't you *lie?*

Conor

I . . . I just don't understand.

Sudden shift.

Old Joy and Conor III

Light upstage of the curtain. In **Joy***'s house. Old* **Joy** *in her chair.*

Conor

Mum, what's that?

Joy

What?

Conor

What's that smell?

Joy

I don't smell anything.

Conor

For God's sake, Mum, of course you do. It's a terrible smell. (*Pause.*) Is it the bins?

Joy

Bins? No!

Conor

It's here. It's in here.

Joy

Oh, what is wrong with you? I wish you would just sit down.

Conor *gets close to her, sniffing.*

Joy

Get away from me! What are you doing?

Conor

Mum you've . . . Oh my god, Jesus. Oh my . . .

Joy

What are you playing at?

Conor

Why didn't you ask someone to help you?

Joy

Help me? I don't need any help!

Conor

Of course you do, Mum. You've shit yourself!

Joy

Excuse me?

Conor

Luka was here all morning. He could have helped you to the bathroom! You need to tell him!

Joy

What are you talking about? Why on earth would I need . . . ?

Conor

Mum! Mum! You've gone to the toilet in your seat. You could've asked Luka to bring you to the toilet . . .

Joy

What you're saying is disgusting!

Conor

I know it's disgusting. I'm going to have to clean you up . . . oh my god!

Joy

You don't have to do anything! I wish you would go!

Conor

Of course I do. I have to do something! I can't just leave you here sitting in it!

Joy

I'm perfectly fine and I don't know what you're getting at!

Conor

Mum! Luka was here all morning, and I've been here for the last hour, I could have brought you to the toilet!

Joy

That's disgusting! What you're saying is disgusting!

Conor

Where are your towels?

Joy

What are you doing? Get out of my cupboard!

Conor

I'm looking for your towels!

Joy

Put my things down!

Conor

I'm looking for your towels! Where are your towels?

Joy

I don't need a towel!

Conor

I need a . . . I need a towel! I found them. I found a towel. Look, you need to ask for help, you can't just sit there!

Joy

I don't need any help! Stop talking to me like I'm some sort of child!

Conor

You needed to go to the toilet and you didn't say it to anyone.

Joy

That's disgusting!

Conor

Your pride got the better of you and now you're sitting in your own shit.

Joy

What you're saying is absolutely appalling, treating your mother like this!

Conor

I'm not treating you like . . . Ok, look, I'm sorry. I'm sorry . . .

Joy

You should be! You should be sorry!

Conor

I'm sorry . . .

Joy

You're being awful to me! You're attacking me! Stop attacking me right now!

Conor

I'm not attacking you!

Joy

Well you are!

Conor

I need to clean you up, ok?

Joy

I don't need to be cleaned up. I don't know what you're at.

Conor

Mum, you need to be cleaned up. I'm gonna put a towel around you . . .

Joy

I wish you would go away . . .

Conor

I wish I could, I wish I could.

Sudden shift.

Young Conor III

Upstage is dark. **Joy** *is downstage of the curtain alone.* **Conor** *is voice only.*

Conor

You're still good for tomorrow?

Joy

Tomorrow? Yes.

Conor

Good. Sandra's really really excited about meeting you.

Joy

Yes of course! I'm excited to meet her.

Conor

Ok good, great, because this is important to me.

Joy

Of course, of course, I'm just so busy with rehearsals and everything I'm just plain exhausted.

Conor

Ok yeah. But you won't cancel on me will you?

Joy

No!

Conor

And it'll be fun.

Joy

Of course it will!

Conor

And even if it's not fun, it's important to me. I know it might not be as important to you but it is to me.

Joy

Conor, is this lunch or some sort of sacrament that I'm taking?

Conor

Sorry. Sorry. It's just . . . sorry . . .

Joy

Don't wait up. Harry's having me over tonight . . .

Conor

Oh? Ok, have fun.

Joy

You'll look after yourself for dinner?

Conor

What time will you be back?

Joy (*becoming frustrated*)

Conor, don't seek certainty in this life. You won't be pleased when you find it. I'll be home . . . at *some* point before lunch tomorrow with your friend . . .

A gradual shift.

Old Joy and Conor IV

Light upstage. **Joy**'s *house.* **Conor** *is there. Old* **Joy** *stands up.* **Joy**, *downstage of the curtain, continues speaking uninterrupted by the scene transition.*

Joy

Now, would you do me a favour and call me a taxi?

Conor

What?

Joy

I'm going to Harry's.

Conor

You . . . you what?

Joy

I already told you I'm going to Harry's.

Conor

Mum, you're not . . .

Joy

Excuse me?

Conor

Mum you're not going to Harry's.

Joy

What?

Conor

Sit down watch some tellie with me ok?

Joy

I'm expected, so do let me pass now . . .

Conor

Sit down Joy, please.

Joy

I'm afraid I can't I'm expected at Harry's.

Conor

Harry's . . . not around anymore.

Joy

What do you mean not around anymore? He called . . .

Conor

He's just not around anymore. You're better off here.

Joy

But I want to go. Stop stopping me.

Conor

Sit please.

Joy

You are a disease that's in my flesh . . .

Conor

That's not very nice.

He gently guides her back into a chair.

Joy

A disease which I must needs call mine!

Conor

Ok. Ok.

Joy

You're a boil.

Conor

Fine. Fine.

Joy

A plague-sore, an embossed carbuncle,
In my corrupted blood.

He leaves, she's left alone for a moment.

Conor

I know, I know. I'll make us something to eat.

Joy

I don't want anything to eat.

Conor

I know you don't. I know. But I do, so join me will you?

Joy

I'm not hungry, I'll eat at Harry's.

Joy *looks around, then quickly stands up and makes for the door.*

Conor

Well I'll make us some soup or something, that way you
can have as much or as little you want. Ok?

Conor *comes in, sees she's up again and heading for the door.*

Conor

No no no no no no Joy you can't! Don't make me go
through this again.

Conor *grabs her.*

Joy

Get away from me!

She slaps him.

Joy

You are a stranger to my heart and me.

Conor *takes her by the shoulders.*

Conor

Right, that's it, come on.

Joy
Let me go, let me go, let me go!

She kicks him in the shin and he lets her go.

Conor
Aghh!

Joy *continues to walk away.* **Conor** *recovers and takes her by the arm. They struggle.*

Conor
You aren't going anywhere! That's the end of it.

Joy (*giving up*)
Fine . . .

She pretends to acquiesce, he relaxes, then suddenly **Joy** *pulls out of* **Conor**'s *grip. She trips and falls on the floor with a thud.*

Lights out upstage. **Joy** *is now alone downstage of the curtain. Music builds.*

Joy
This heart
Shall break into a hundred thousand flaws
Or ere I'll weep!

Lightning, thunder. Rain. **Conor**'s *face up on the curtain behind her.*

The Storm (Part 2 – Thunder and Lightning)

Conor (*into the camera,* **Joy**'s *POV*)
'Dear Joy. I'm really looking forward to going travelling together this summer. Dad didn't seem so sure about it. He seems to think you'll be busy even though I told him we had planned it. I was wondering, if it's not too much trouble, can you call him and tell him?' . . .

I read that now and I think . . . what a stupid little kid! So stupid to believe a thing you said. I mean . . . you didn't have to take me on trips or whatever. But why did you tell me you would? Did you believe that stuff you told me? Or did you always know it was bullshit? Just some story?

'I don't want to hassle you, but I also don't know if you're getting my letters or they're getting lost in the post. So, if you could let me know that would be great.'

There were dozens of these. In their envelopes. Most of them unopened. You didn't even read them. I was writing to a ghost.

Thunder, wind and lighting. **Joy** *is upstage of the gauze now and is in the action.*

Joy

Blow, winds, and crack your cheeks! rage! blow!
You cataracts and hurricanes, spout
Till you have drench'd our steeples, drown'd the cocks!
You sulphurous and thought-executing fires,
Vaunt-couriers to oak-cleaving thunderbolts

Thunder. Envelopes fall from the sky onto **Joy**.

Liam

O nuncle, court holy-water in a dry
house is better than this rain-water out o' door.
Good nuncle, in, and ask thy daughters' blessing:
here's a night pities neither wise man nor fool.
Singe my white head!

A total lurching shift to a new reality. The storm sound is replaced by a trickle of water. **Liam** *is helping* **Joy** *bathe. She recites gently to* **Liam**, *and he back to her, while he washes and dries her hair.*

Joy

And thou, all-shaking thunder,
Smite flat the thick rotundity o' the world!
Crack nature's moulds, an germens spill at once,
That make ingrateful man!

Liam
Alas, sir, are you here? things that love night
Love not such nights as these; the wrathful skies
Gallow the very wanderers of the dark,
And make them keep their caves:

A lurching shift, **Joy** *gets under the towel and speaks directly to a camera. We see her face projected which is suddenly old, as it was in the mirror earlier. She speaks to the camera.*

Joy (*to a camera*)
Rumble thy bellyful! Spit, fire! spout, rain!
Nor rain, wind, thunder, fire, are my daughters:
I tax not you, you elements, with unkindness;
I never gave you kingdom, call'd you children,

Conor's *face comes up on the downstage curtain.* **Joy** *stops. As though she can hear him for a moment.*

Conor (*into a camera,* **Joy**'s *POV*)
And here you are again
You've got everyone running around after you.
Terrified. Trying to please you.
Doling out punishments and little rewards
I felt it, the second I set foot in here
Like a kid again
There's nothing new here
You only ever existed in these stories you tell yourself.

Joy *listens to* **Conor**. *Looking at the camera as if looking at him.*

Conor (*into camera,* **Joy**'s *POV*)
You're a black hole
You're sucking us all in after you

Conor *video out. He pulls on his jacket and starts looking for* **Joy** *in the rain.*

Conor
Joy? Joy? Mum?

Joy (*on screen*) *looks around. She is hearing her name called. Throws off the towel. Video out. She is lost in the storm for a moment and* **Liam** *finds her.*

Liam (*sheltering*)
The reason why the seven stars are no more than seven is a pretty reason.

Joy
Because they are not eight?

They laugh.

Joy (*to the camera*)
And the King never thought about his youngest daughter again!
And the King never thought about his youngest daughter.

Liam *helps* **Joy** *lie down on the towel on the floor. A camera is held above her, shooting her face. Onto the towel, around her head, we see colourful synapses firing.*

Liam (*as he lowers her onto the towel*)
Good nuncle, in, and ask thy daughter's blessing
Ask thy daughter's blessing.

Joy (*to the camera*)
And the King never thought about his youngest daughter again.
And the King never thought about his youngest daughter.

Liam (*as he exits*)
Ask her blessing
Ask her blessing!

Joy (*gently, under* **Conor**'s *speech*)
All is storms. All is chaos. Your gods can't help you. All is storms. Your mother can't help you. All is storms.
We're blowing out.
We're returning to our preferred state. Nothing.

Conor (*into camera, cross faded over the above*)
'Dear Joy. I'm very sorry if I said the wrong thing or if I didn't

express myself well enough the last time I visited. I just want you
to know that I think you're wonderful and that you're very
talented and that I always love seeing you and meeting your
friends.'

I was a kid writing that to you. A fucking kid. You treated
me terribly and I was always the one apologising. Always
saying 'sorry'.

Curtain is pulled back.

The Storm (Part 3 – Blown Out)

We are back in the nursing home. Old **Joy** *is played by the puppet.*
Conor*'s video disappears he continues his speech uninterrupted by*
the scene transition. He is now speaking to the puppet version of
Joy*.*

Conor
. . . you made me feel like I'm nothing. You made me feel
like I don't exist. And that's a bad feeling. It's wrong and I
want to be done with it. I am done with it. I'm done with
you.

Conor *turns away. Puts his coat on.*

Joy
You do me wrong.

Conor *pauses.*

Joy
You do me wrong!

Conor
I do *you* wrong?

Liam *stops him. Listen!*

Joy
You do me wrong to take me out of the grave.

Liam *goes to the book and finds the right page.*

Joy
> Thou art a soul in bliss; but I am bound
> Upon a wheel of fire, that mine own tears
> Do scald like molten lead.

Liam *gives the right page in the book to* **Conor**. **Conor**'s *not sure.*
Liam *presses him. Pause.*

Conor (*reading*)
> Sir, do you know me?

Joy
> Pray, do not mock me:
> I am a very foolish fond old man,
> Methinks I should know you,
> Yet I am doubtful for I am mainly ignorant
> Where I did lodge last night. Do not laugh at me;
> For, as I am a man, I think this lady
> To be my child Cordelia.

Conor
> And so I am, I am.

Joy
> Be your tears wet? yes, 'faith. I pray, weep not:
> If you have poison for me, I will drink it.
> I know you do not love me
> You have cause.

Conor
> I do. Fuck you.

Joy
> Pray you now, forget and forgive:
> I am old and foolish.

Conor
> Yes. You're forgiven.

Pause.

Joy
> Fine. Fine. But off book for tomorrow, yes?

Epilogue

Carers exit. **Liam** *exits.* **Conor** *pulls the gauze curtain across the scene and exits. Old* **Joy** *on her own, sitting in her chair. Lights flickering like synapses. Pulsing, lightning, degrading.*

A final flicker. Blackout.

For a complete listing of
Methuen Drama titles, visit:
www.bloomsbury.com/drama

Follow us on X and keep up to date with
our news and publications
@MethuenDrama